THE MUSEUM OF

CLEAR IDEAS

෨

POETRY BY DONALD HALL

Exiles and Marriages (1955)

The Dark Houses (1958)

A Roof of Tiger Lilies (1964)

The Alligator Bride (1969)

The Yellow Room (1971)

The Town of Hill (1975)

Kicking the Leaves (1978)

The Happy Man (1986)

The One Day (1988)

Old and New Poems (1990)

THE MUSEUM

OF CLEAR

IDEAS

∾

Donald Hall

· *Ticknor & Fields* ·

NEW YORK

1993

For information about permission to reproduce selections
from this book, write to Permissions, Ticknor & Fields,
215 Park Avenue South, New York, New York 10003.

Library of Congress Cataloging-in-Publication Data

Hall, Donald, 1928.
The museum of clear ideas / Donald Hall.
p.   cm.
ISBN 0-395-65236-7
I. Title.
PS3515.A3152M86   1993
811'.54—dc20   92-23328
CIP
Printed in the United States of America

BP   10   9   8   7   6   5   4   3   2   1

Book design by Anne Chalmers

A number of poems previously appeared in the following pub-
lications: *Agni:* The Ninth Inning. *The Atlantic Monthly:* When
the young husband. *Boston Phoenix:* In the name of; Camilla,
never ask; Drusilla informs; Dr. Zero's Reproof. *Boulevard:* The
Sixth Inning; The Seventh Inning. *Cream City Review:* When I
was young. *The Gettysburg Review:* The Fourth Inning; The
Fifth Inning; The Eighth Inning. *Harvard Review:* Nunc est
bibendum. *The Iowa Review:* Another Elegy. *New American
Writing:* The First Inning; The Second Inning. *New England
Review:* "Extra Innings." *The New Republic:* Let us meditate the
virtue. *The Paris Review:* various poems from "The Museum of
Clear Ideas." *Partisan Review:* two poems from "The Museum
of Clear Ideas." *Pequod:* Don't be afraid; Nothing, my aging
Flaccus; Let engine cowling. *The Plum Review:* excerpt from
"The Museum of Clear Ideas." *Southern Humanities Review:* three
poems from "The Museum of Clear Ideas."

CONTENTS

Extra Innings

Notes   119

for Jane

ANOTHER

ELEGY

•

In Memory of
William Trout

"O God!" thoughte I, "that madest kynde,
Shal I noon other weyes dye?
Wher Joves woll me stellefye,
Or what thing may this sygnifye? . . ."

— Geoffrey Chaucer, *Hous of Fame*

The task and potential greatness of mortals reside
in their ability to produce things which are at home
in everlastingness.

— Hannah Arendt, *The Human Condition*

Both one and many; in the brown baked features
The eyes of a familiar compound ghost . . .

— T. S. Eliot, "Little Gidding"

It rained all night on the remaining elms. April soaked
through night loam into sleep. This morning, rain delays
above drenched earth. Whitethroated sparrows shake
wet from their feathers, singing in the oak, while fog
snags like lambswool on Kearsarge. The Blackwater River
runs high. The blacksnake budges in his hole, resurrecting
from winter's coma.
                    Now green will start from stubble
and horned pout fatten. By the pond, pussywillows
will labor awake to trudge from darkness and cold
through April's creaking gate.
                    Bill Trout remains
fixed in a long box where we left him, a dozen years ago.

                              ◆

July, nineteen sixty: Three friends with their families
visited Bill at his Maine cabin secluded among scrub pines —
setting up tents, joking, frying pickerel in cool dusk.

Only Bill was divorced, drinking all night, living alone
on his shabby acre. Drunk the whole week, he recited
Milton's syllables of lament, interrupting our argument,
told Nazarene parables, and wept for his friends
and their children. While the rest of us dove from a dock
or played badminton with our wives, Bill paced
muttering, smoking his Lucky Strikes. Later the rest
divorced and paced.
                    We fished the river for horned pout,
Bill standing with a joint by the dam, watching the warm
water thick with fish, black bodies packed, flapping

and contending to breathe. Dropping hooks without bait,
we pulled up the horny, loricate fish, then flipped them
on grass to shrivel as we watched and joked, old
friends together. Continually sloshed, Bill proclaimed
that life was shit, death was shit — even *shit* was *shit*.

◆

Idaho made him, Pocatello of hobos and freightyards —
clangor of iron, fetor of coalsmoke. With his brothers
he listened for the Mountain Bluebird as he dropped worms
into the Snake River, harvesting catfish for a Saturday
supper in the nineteen thirties.
                              Two Sisters of the Sacred Heart
cossetted him when he strayed from the boys' flock
to scan the unchanging dactyls of Ovid. Landowska set out
the Goldberg Variations on a hand-wound Victrola.

When he was fifteen he stayed home from fishing to number
feet that promenaded to a Union Pacific tune, ABAB
pentameters. At the university his teacher the disappointed
novelist nodded his head — in admiration, envy, and pity —
while Bill sat late at a yellow dormitory desk, daydreaming
that his poems lifted through night sky to become stars
fixed in heaven, as Keats's poems rose from Hampstead
lanes and talks with Hunt and Haydon.
                              When he considered
the cloth, Bill saw himself martyred. The ambition
of priest and poet! — innocent, and brainless as a shark.

◆

Sculptors make models for touch; singers raise voices
to the possible voice; basketball players improvise
humors of levitation. They jump, carve, and sing in plain
air as we do dreaming.
                              Because emblems of every calling
measure its aspiration, the basketball player shoots
three hundred freethrows before breakfast; the mezzo
exists in service to the sound she makes, without eating
or loving except for song, selfish and selfless together;
the novice imagines herself healing a dozen Calcuttas
as Mother Teresa smiles from a gold cloud, and violates
holiness by her daydream of holiness.
                              Bill Trout
woke up, the best mornings of his life — without debilities
of hangover, without pills or panic — to practice joy
at four o'clock dawn: to test words, to break them down
and build again, patient to construct immovable objects
of art by the pains of intelligent attention — remaining
alert or awake to nightmare.
                              But the maker of bronzes
dies decapitated in the carwreck; the whitefaced mime
dozes tied to the wheelchair; the saint babbles and drools;
carcinoma refines chemist, farmer, wino, professor, poet,
imbecile, and banker into a passion of three nerves
and a feeding tube.
                              At the Bayside Hospice Bill's body
heaved as it worked for air; IVs dripped; bloody phlegm
boiled from the hole punched like a grommet in his throat.

◆

Another fisherman writes me: "A man's death is his own; you take Bill's death away, for public tears." I remember Bill depressed, drinking double Manhattans straight up, taunting himself: "Compassion's flack! Elmer Gantry of Guggenheim grief!" In Coleridge's *Notebooks*, he underlined: "Poetry — excites us to artificial feelings — callous to real ones."

Commonly Bill recited, from John 14, "I go to make a place," then shrugged and sang the Wobbly hymn, "You'll eat pie in the sky by and by — when you die." After reciting Thomas Hardy, he went on to mimic Oliver.

Two years after the Maine summer, he worked for SNCC in Alabama, in a cadre of Christians and Jews, beaten bloody and jailed, declaiming Amos as gospel of anger and love.

Angry he married again; loving he wrote "Selma with Hellfire."

A decade after, as we sat late in a bare Port Townsend room, bossily I reminded him to eat the wax-paper'd hamburger cooling by his ashtray. Bill delivered a line, in his voice as lush as an old Shakespearean's: "Ohhhh . . . to think of the mornings I've waked with a cold cheeseburger beside me!"

He walked into water and out again; he woke in the drunktank heaving; he trembled after electroshock; he made the poems.

◆

If ambition is innocent, nevertheless it impairs those it possesses, not to mention their irretrievable children.

In the interstices of alcohol and woe, Bill vibrated
awake to a room that surged, shook, and altered shape.
He secreted vowel-honey in images dangling from prepositions;
he praised survival.

     When he finished his sojourn
at McLean, where Very and Lowell had paced before him;
when Margaret left him, removing their daughter, and Bill
declared bankruptcy; when he was unable for five years
to take Communion — he drank two Guggenheims and snorted
an NEA. He quoted Amos: ". . . as if a man fled from a lion
and a bear met him."

     From his house in Oakland, USIS
flew him to Prague, then home to detox. Once I visited him
just back from drying out, shuffling from chair to table
like a ninety-year-old, shaking as he tried to light
his Lucky, barely able to speak.

     Then in middle age
he fell in love again. He listened again to Chaucer
and recited Spenser's refrain as he stood by the Thames,
holding his Hindu love by the hand; or walking arm in arm
by a lake where Wordsworth walked;

       or, happy in Delhi,
reading the Gita, he breathed each morning India's fetid
exhausted air, filling his notebook in warm dawn
as parrots flashed and his throat opened with gold
vowels, line after beautiful line, all the last summer.

       ◆

The week before he died he handed me a clutch of poems.
Speechless, syllables occluded in his throat, he raised
a yellow pad and wrote, "That's it." Eyes protruded
from bone sockets; neck cords strained; trunk heaved
as he looked for his love who gazed out the window
of the room, bare except for a crucifix, downward to the bay
and the brown edges of March.

                          After he died Reba gave me
his Modern Library Dickinson, in which editors corrected
the poet's lines. I imagine Bill in Eugene, penciling,
neat in the margin, restorations of Amherst.

                                 Each year
his death grows older. Outside this house, past Kearsarge
changing from pink and lavender through blue and white
to green, public language ridicules "eager pursuit of honor."

Do I tell lies? ". . . in middle age he fell in love . . ."
Did he never again tremble from chair to table? At night
Bill delivered his imagination and study to *Laverne
and Shirley*, laughing when a laughtrack bullied him
to laugh — while Reba groaned an incredulous Bengali groan —
in order not to drink.

                        Yet again he walked in a blue
robe in detox, love's anguish and anger walking beside him.

◆

It is twelve Aprils since we buried him. Now dissertation-
salt preserves *The Collected Poems of William Trout*

like Lenin. Here is another elegy in the tradition
of mourning and envy, love and self-love — as another morning
delivers rain on the fishbone leaves of the rotted year.
Again I measure the poems Bill Trout left on the shore
of his scattery life: quatrains that scrubbed Pocatello
clean, numbers of nightmare and magic, late songs in love
with Reba and vowels — his lifelines that hooked and landed
himself and his own for his book.
                                    But if a new fixed star
resurrects Bill's words who labored and excelled, not even
Chaucer's or Ovid's accomplishment — "Joves woll me stellyfye" —
will revise electrodes, jail, and death at fifty.
Bill Trout is incorrigible, like the recidivist blacksnake,
sparrow, and high water that turn and return in April's
versions — cycles of the same, fish making fish —
                                                    "unless,"
Bill dying, shriveled and absolved, wrote on a yellow
pad, "Jesus who walked from the tomb has made us a place."

◆

BASEBALL

◆

1. I would like to explain baseball to
Kurt Schwitters, Merz-poet and artist,
whose work was clothing, office, bedroom,
and carapace, who glued together
assemblages of ordinary
things — cigarette wrappers, bus tickets,
ads — first to make collage, and then to
inhabit. I would like to linger
with Schwitters in the Fenway bleachers,

2. explaining baseball. But, as poets
tell us, the man is dead, and I — call
me K.C. — lack his German, much less
death's German. Well, there are nine players
on a baseball team, so to speak, and
there are nine innings, with trivial
exceptions like extra-inning games
and games shortened by rain or darkness,
by riot, hurricane, earthquake, or

3. the Second Law of Thermodynam-
ics. Rilke feared the death of the sun;
then we exploded the sun. The Merz-
collagist expired in England, of
emphysema originally
contracted during poverty and
inflation, when he smoked the deutschemark.
Rilke died of leukemia, his
blood clarified to spiritual

4. water. When Jennifer walks down the
driveway, absently posting letters
in the mailbox or strolling across
the road to water the chickens, I
lean after her narrow waist — the swell
undulant above it, below it
the smooth slender outcurving outswoop —
the way July's daylily buds tip
south from Ragged's green hill, following

5. the risen sun, and swell to erupt
orange. Tonight, after baseball, she
looks Chinese, skin under her eyes puffed
from her morning tears. As she totters,
she touches bookcase and tabletop
with the tips of dubious fingers.
Depression is the blood's own journey,
by its own map. There is only one
thing to do; happily we do it.

6. From home plate to the pitcher's rubber,
as the actress said to the bishop,
takes sixty feet and six inches. Of
course you will recognize Being: It
looks just like Nothingness except that
it wears a striped Thai-silk four-in-hand.
As the poet says, "Words cannot tell,
cannot express . . . Words falter . . . Words are
inadequate to describe . . ." Poets

7. woo the unspeakable to their desks,
listening to radio baseball.
Meantime the cells or constituent
molecules go on sunning themselves
in the pure daylight of unconscious
punning and dancing, now slowing down,
now jetting Cambridge blue electrons —
the enterprise of ongoingness.
This condition resembles baseball

8. in its laboratory method
or purity, physics of nine times
nine times nine times nine. We hanged three deer
behind the new 7-Eleven
beside lions Flaubert crucified.
I am not interested in words
without sentences, or sentences
without meaning. Every meaningless
sentence says the same thing. Igitur,

9. they pave the green mountain for progress
while they grow hairy vert chemicals
into grass cement for the diamond
and Newfound Lake newly obscured by
sawtooth-shingled condominia
at x thousand thousand dollars each
to prohibit view of the wind's lake.
Kurt, when the pitcher makes a false start,
the runners move up: It is a balk.

1. When I wake each morning, each morning
points itself like a dog at the fowl
of baseball. My father who adored
the game died on the year's shortest day,
on December the twenty-second
at six-twenty P.M., long after
sundown. When we buried him, Christmas
Eve, the day was already longer.
His hands were long and always busy:

2. like dachshunds, like the wooden carvings
in old churches, like bowls of cashew
nuts. Although Cincinnati's ballpark
is symmetrical and horrific,
its execution of the German-
American wurst is exceeded
only by Milwaukee's. When I first
wrote about rising and pointing, I
arrived instead at the bird of work.

3. Baseball is not my work. It is my
walk in the park, my pint of bitter,
my Agatha Christie or Zane Grey —
release of the baby animal's
energy into the jungle gym
of a frivolous concentration.
Also I dictate letters between
pitches — as I observe the Red Sox
or whatever game's on satellite.

4. Who can say what his or her work is?
I write out these tentative verses
— K.C. at the Desk, Mudville at bat,
last of the ninth — working in the dark
morning while a cat climbs on my lap
nibbling at pen and paper. For sure,
my pleasure is an habitual
recreational tapping at blocks
of the language, absentmindedly,

5. even when "there is no language there"
(Jenny says) — frustration frustrated
by counting on fingers of almost
two hands. Don't forget, Kurt: Use two hands
when you catch the ball, and don't ignore
the starved cat. In the multiplying
gossip of cells, catch the Sprechstimme
of the spheres. A baseball is a sphere,
or near enough. The pitiful quarks

6. turn charming: meiosis, mitosis,
off and on. It was light and motion
before Moses was, before you are,
and I am. Entropy contracts cold;
density implodes: Let there be light
and chattering membranes of discourse.
Rain for seven innings at Fenway
Park, mist and drizzle, drizzle and mist
on umbrellas in front-row boxes:

7. Most of us withdrew to remote seats
under cover while the straight youthful
men of the outfield splashed through puddles,
mudsliding for fly balls. After six
innings and an hour's wait, the umpires
called the game off, tied one to one. We
struggled wetly out to Kenmore Square
after a game without issue. Young
ballplayers partied and slept, to rise

8. tomorrow for a doubleheader
starting at five-thirty. All night long,
asleep, I practiced how to focus
my eyes to catch the light rain falling
slant against green grass and uniformed
boys: rain like time in dowels of light.
K.C.'s omnium-gatherum (in
New English we call it "town dump") weds
the East Side to Langton Street. I dreamed

9. of old Ezra Pound after meeting
Olga Rudge at Orono, Maine. A
peregrine falcon flew in and out
of my dream. Just twenty-five years back,
I interviewed Pound as he entered
the house of silence. But the dream bird?
The next day I understood: I felt
troubled about another old man:
Henry Moore wheelchaired at Perry Green.

1. Alexander, first over the wall,
collapsed battered by stones. Instantly
the Macedonian companions
gathered their shields over his body
and these athletes of honor and brawn
withstood repeated iron assault —
to defend, to survive, to triumph.
When the king's wound healed, he divided
the known world among his companions.

2. At the center of a baseball, Kurt,
is ten pounds of cat intestine, packed
into a tiny marble-sized sphere.
While I write "Baseball," Prudence the cat
rubs at my ankles to inform me
that nothing whatever bothers her.
Jennifer and I make love at night;
afterward, happiness continues,
as if the radio, turned on low

3. at three A.M., told about baseball
all night long in Japanese or Spanish,
with crowd noises the same as Fenway.
The next morning, as Jenny pauses
by the kitchen sink and looks idly
out the window, I gaze at her ass;
then she squeezes an orange: Its bright
gelatinous membranes rupture to
fill her blue cup with sunny ichor.

4. The ship made twenty-five knots into
a fifty-knot wind over hot gulf
water. I climbed to the topmost deck,
tilting my weight into the hot wind,
poising my heavy body into
the wind's weight, pulling myself along
rails with both hands to push against wind
that scudded black clouds into blackness
with the moon down and few stars showing.

5. Wind flattened my beard and my nostrils.
Wind gathered my shout and shuffled it.
It is ecstasy beyond pleasure
to watch Jennifer squeeze orange juice.
All night the kitten walked back and forth
on top of us, biting and poking.
Meantime the old cat hissed and added
new disloyalties to her lifelist,
as when the Dodgers left Ebbets Field.

6. So the new dog's pet is the kitten.
All day she hurls herself at his huge
muzzle, bigger than she is, her mouth
wide open and her claws stretched. He snaps
without biting, love bites; she pauses
in her fury to lick his jaws clean.
Then she hides — to leap from her secret
branch onto the great boa of his
wagging magnificent golden tail.

7. All winter aged ballplayers try
rehearsing their young manhood, running
and throwing in Florida's sunshine;
they remain old. In my sixtieth
year I wake fretting over some new
failure. Meeting an old friend's new wife,
I panicked and was rude. Or I ache
mildly, feeling some careless anger
with my son I cannot push away.

8. The bodies of major league baseball
players are young. We age past the field
so quickly; we diminish, watching
over decades, observing the young
as they dodder. The old cat hisses
at the kitten and pokes the new dog;
her life is ruined and she declines
bitterly toward death. At night she purrs
briefly, lying restored on our bed.

9. The leg is the dancer and the mouth
the sculptor. The tongue models vowels
or chisels consonants. Pause, pitch, pace,
length, and volume patine a surface
of shapes that the mouth closes over.
Behind our listening lips, working
the throat's silent machine, one muscle
shuts on/off/on/off: the motionless
leg of the word that leaps in the world.

1. As the moment's vowel rolls itself
out, mind entertains intelligence
for body's sake. Word-skin and muscle-
shape dance to the corporal music
of sententia or anecdote.
Syntax is sinew. In the aroused
mouth, sweet juices accumulate verbs,
adjectives, and nouns lolling in luxe,
calme, et volupté like Miami.

2. In nineteen seventy-three, Dock said
that pitcher and poet were up to
the same tricks. "All I'm trying to do,"
he said, "is fool 'em." When you expect
robinsegg blue, I suppose, you get
rubberized cement instead. Always
remember, Kurt, that Sandy Koufax
spoke of pitching baseball as "the art
of intimidation." To instill

3. fear, what do poets do? Robert Frost
said that the thing was to *score,* to *win,*
and his ambitious or murderous
eyes frightened anyone who took them
in. Sixty, he played vicious softball.
The pitcher stares at the catcher's mitt
and appears, Kurt, to glare once in the
batter's direction. The batter's eyes
concentrate on body, arm, and ball.

4. John Tudor was annoyed by the press
after his second World Series win
in nineteen eighty-five. For Tudor,
success's discomfort reversed it.
Heraclitus affirmed reversals
and the truest poem exposes
itself in a fury of self-love
and flagellation. In the last game
John Tudor's team never got it up.

5. If the destination is always
a lie, because (1) we cannot stop,
(2) there is no *there* there, and (3) there
is no (3), is the journey also
mendacious? Doubtless, conceptual
propositions make no never-mind
and K.C.'s traveling metaphor
dies the usual death. Let us go
back to gazing at Jennifer's shorts.

6. This poem is necessarily
dedicated to Gerald Burns, the
commissioner of "Baseball." Former
dispensations necessitated
sequences of eighty sonnets, then
one further. When Lefty Gomez died,
Bill Dickey remembered a story:
Gomez shook off his signs as Jimmy
Foxx stood at the plate; at the mound, Bill

7. asked what his pitcher *wanted*. "Nothing,"
said Gomez. "I thought he might get tired
of waiting and go away." Walking
on the island of Inishbofin,
eight miles into the Atlantic off
Galway, we strangers met an old blind
woman in black who, just to be safe,
scratched a cross in the dirt path with her
blackthorn stick. That day on the island

8. there was a rumor that a boatload
of tourists from Spain would drop anchor
in the bay. Annie Morin fixed us
with blank eyes and asked: "Be ye the Moors?"
When Wade Boggs took BP he heard them
chanting "Margo," and as he finished
showering and climbed onto the team
bus, a small boy yelled "Margo" at the
window. With a single-edge razor,

9. a Gem, I sliced the printed sheets of
balsa; I glued; I stretched lavender
tissue paper over frail wing-ribs;
I sanded propellers. But the glued
ribs and struts sprung and the paper tore.
My planes like my baseballs never flew —
or my best fastball *flew* over the
backstop; I struck out; I dropped the ball:
Airplanes crashed on my feckless sandlot.

1. Kurt, last night Dwight Evans put it all
together, the way you made collage,
with an exemplary catch followed
by an assist at first base, a hit
in the seventh inning for the tie,
and another in the last of the
ninth to pull it out at Fenway Park
and win the game. The madness method
of "Baseball" gathers bits and pieces

2. of ordinary things — like bleacher
ticket stubs, used Astroturf, Fenway
Frank wrappers, yearbooks, and memory —
to paste them onto the bonkers grid
of the page. I stood at the workbench
after school and all day on weekends
— and I stand there still, in the gloomy
cellar on Ardmore Street, cutting and
gluing, my tongue protruding from my

3. lips, and nothing flies. When my daughter —
bored at thirteen by the grown-up talk
at the fancy picnic outside the
theater in Stratford, Ontario —
remarked frequently on the paddle-
boats skimming the lake ("Oh, look!" "That looks
like fun!" "I wonder where they start from."),
I understood: I said, "Let's go find
the dock or whatever and rent one."

4. Her face livened up, but she was smart:
As we walked toward the pier together,
she asked: "Are you certain you want to
do this, or are you doing it just
to be mean?" In nineteen thirty-eight,
the hurricane lifted Aunt Clara's
cottage at Silver Sands and carried
it twenty yards to deposit it
in a salt meadow; the tidal wave

5. overwhelmed the Thimble Island where
Uncle Arthur lived. When rain started
in the second inning at Fenway
Park, it drizzled on umbrellas raised
in boxes by the field. Most of us
climbed to remote seats back under the
overhang to watch the (I wrote this
before, back in the second inning)
puddles pocked by raindrops. In the lights

6. we made out straight up-and-down falling
pencil lines of rain that the pitchers
squinted through to see the catchers' signs;
batters peered to watch how the ball spun.
After six innings it rained harder
and the umpire suspended play — game
tied three to three — then called it an hour
later. We struggled wetly out from
a game without issue. The young men

7. partied and slept, to make tomorrow's
doubleheader at five. All night I
slept and woke practicing — obsessive
even in sleep, just as I bully
notes into lines — how the slow rain fell
like time measured in vertical light.
When I was a child, Connecticut
of the thirties and forties, we drove
to Ebbets Field or the Polo Grounds,

8. a couple of hours down the newly
constructed or incomplete parkways
to Brooklyn especially, dense with
its tiny park and passionate crowd.
After Billy Herman brilliantly
stopped a ground ball and flipped to Pee Wee
for the force, I turned immediate
attention to a vendor and my
father thought I missed the lucky play.

9. While that was happening, Kurt, I guess
you left Germany for Norway. Good.
As I thought about Curt (sic) Davis,
you were building a Merz-apartment.
I watched the first game of the nineteen
forty-one World Series in the Bronx,
when Joe Gordon took Curt Davis deep
and we lost three to two, unable
to rally back. Then the long drive home.

1. Sometime, Kurt, you ought to come along
to Danbury Elementary
School when I umpire a softball game.
I call balls and strikes, safe and out, foul
and fair. When I blow a call, I make
it up on the next one. Once when I
intoned "Strike one!" a small batter said,
"Hey, that's your 'Casey at the Bat' voice,
Mr. Hall." (I dislike it, having

2. a poetry voice — but I have one.)
Danbury goes through the sixth grade, and
the best game of the year is the last,
when the sixth grade plays the P.T.O.
reinforced by teachers. Serious
athleticism and revenge combine
to dissipate in the ethical
disorder of prejudiced calls by
an undisinterested umpire.

3. Before we left Spring Glen Grammar School
for high school, the eighth grade played hardball.
I tried out for catcher, knowing that,
aside from a good first-string player,
nobody wanted to wear the mask.
They cut me anyway, and I slunk
off to my familiar province of
tears, failure, and humiliation
where I lived until Harvard College.

4. Sometimes I take naps as shallow as
puddles on cracked sidewalks in Spring Glen
after a summer shower when sun
will lift the dampness soon and restore
dryness to white cement. And sometimes
I nap the rare nap as profound as
the Pacific Ocean, where fathoms
of fault steam from a crack in the deep
floor: Napoleon! Napoleon!

5. After fifty years of images
and symbols (watch out, kids; here comes a
symbol), it is difficult to keep
oneself head-bent-down to the language
only, as if language were a grid
for athletes, Kurt, as in parts of speech.
If a coincidence of noises
suggests the possibility of
interjecting a French emperor

6. onto a suburb confounded with
an ocean composed of shifting plates
and geological moral terms
multiplied by alliteration,
what have we gained except, perhaps, the
grid's distracted polymorphous joy
in evasion? I insinuate
notions despite my resolution,
of many years, to remain aloof

7. from disputes over the usefulness
of this method of generation
or that. I know from experience
that the matter of least import is
what you *think* you are doing. Still, I
exercise control by not making
public, by crossing out, perhaps to
some degree by concealing myself —
but mostly by keeping my silence.

8. Thus K.C. becomes Napoleon,
Nap Lajoie's first name. In the Book of
Dead Cats, dishes of Nine Lives Super
Supper petrify. A permanent
odor of tomcat establishes
ownership in the next world of twelve
volumes of the *OED*, snapshots
breathe three times a year, and the armchair's
clawmarks reify practices of

9. rodent control listed in the Book
of Dead Mice. Soft columns of tanned skin
descend from her pink shorts this morning:
Jennifer's. I stare happily at
linen that covers her slender hips,
at her thighs and knees. What good fortune
to touch Jennifer's limbs — delicate,
supple, smooth, and skinny as a deer's —
that twist with a grown woman's passion.

1. Baseball, I warrant, is not the whole
occupation of the aging boy.
Far from it: There are cats and roses;
there is her water body. She fills
the skin of her legs up, like water;
under her blouse, water assembles,
swelling lukewarm; her mouth is water,
her cheekbones cool water; water flows
in her rapid hair. I drink water

2. from her body as she walks past me
to open a screen door, as she bends
to weed among herbs, or as she lies
beside me at five in the morning
in submarine light. Curt Davis threw
a submarine ball, terrifying
to right-handed batters. Another
pleasure, thoroughly underrated,
is micturition, which is even

3. commoner than baseball. It begins
by announcing itself more slowly
and less urgently than sexual
desire, but (confusingly) in the
identical place. Ignorant men
therefore on occasion confuse beer-
drinking with love; but I have discussed
adultery elsewhere. We allow
this sweet release to commence itself,

4. addressing a urinal perhaps,
perhaps poised over a white toilet
with feet spread wide and head tilted back:
oh, what delicious permission! what
luxury of letting go! what luxe
yellow curve of mildest ecstasy!
Granted we may not compare it to
poignant and crimson bliss, it is as
voluptuous as rain all night long

5. after baseball in August's parch. The
jade plant's trunk, as thick as a man's wrist,
urges upward thrusting from packed dirt,
with Chinese vigor spreading limbs out
that bear heavy leaves — palpable, dark,
juicy, green, profound: They suck, the way
bleacher fans claim inhabitants of
box seats do. The Fourth of July we
exhaust stars from sparklers in the late

6. twilight. We swoop ovals of white-gold
flame, making quick signatures against
an imploding dark. The five-year-old
girl kisses the young dog goodbye and
chases the quick erratic kitten.
When she returns in a few years as
a tall shy girl, she will come back to
a dignified spreading cat and a
dog ash-gray on the muzzle. Sparklers

7. expel quickly this night of farewell:
If they didn't burn out, they wouldn't
be beautiful. Kurt, may I hazard
an opinion on expansion? Last
winter meetings, the major leagues (al-
ready meager in ability,
scanty in starting pitchers) voted
to add two teams. Therefore minor league
players will advance all too quickly,

8. with boys in the bigs who wouldn't have
made double-A forty years ago.
Directors of player personnel
will search like poets scrambling in old
notebooks for unused leftover lines,
but when was the last time anyone
cut back when he or she could expand?
Kurt, I get the notion that you were
another who never discarded

9. *anything*, a keeper from way back.
You smoked cigarettes, in inflation-
times rolled from chopped-up banknotes, billions
inhaled and exhaled as cancerous
smoke. When commerce woke, Merz was awake.
If you smoked a cigar, the cigar
band discovered itself glued into
collage. Ongoing life became the
material of Kurtschwittersball.

1. Kurt, terror is merely the thesis:
Ten years later the guerrilla chief
swears himself in as President for
Life, appointing Commando Plastique
his Minister for Health and Welfare.
Meanwhile former Emperor Pluto
wags his tail at the Zurich Hilton,
attended by his Secretary,
Miss Universe-*und*-Swiss-Bankaccount.

2. However, Kurt, we must inform you
with regret (you will not be surprised)
that The Committee of Reconcil-
iation finds itself unable
to attend the ceremonies, nor
will it observe the Riviera
reunion of the secret police:
The peacemakers have been moldering
in their mass grave for a decade. I

3. cherish the photograph on my wall,
Kurt, where you embrace Bambino Babe
Ruth (Tokyo, nineteen twenty-eight).
Photography's dolor is common:
We are forever older than our
photographs. Even a Polaroid —
by the time the fish of the image
has swum to the surface and settled
into its fins and fortunes for all

4. eternity — measures another
sixty seconds fading toward the grave.
Baseball, like sexual intercourse
and art, stops short, for a moment, the
indecent continuous motion
of time forward, implying our death
and imminent decomposition.
Did you ever marry the bottle?
I married Scotch when I was forty.

5. For two years we kept house together.
She constructed pale renewable
joy when twilight was summer; she was
impassive, agreeable, faithful,
forgiving; she was church and castle,
princess and dragon, Eden and Elm
Street, hell and heaven poured together.
If it were not God's will, the baseball
would disintegrate when the pitcher

6. touched it. Grace before dinner implores
food to remain among visible
things: Only His will sustains peapods.
Flying over China we saw base-
ball diamonds in the sun. Guangzhou and
Shenyang, the smallest of our cities,
each kept four million people. We pale
anomalous tall phantoms with big
noses walked at night in the glow from

7. small shops among the polloi that roiled
multitudinousness everywhere.
In Chengdu at night the scroll sellers
played flashlights over their wares — bamboo,
dragons, snapdragons — that hung from ropes
strung between poplars. In the full moon
the fox walks on snow, black prints of fox;
but the chicken's head has migrated
to the pigsty already. Oink. Oink.

8. Baseball in the winter is our dream's
retrospective summer, and even
(D. V.) the summer of prospect, game
perfectly mental that we control
by the addition of our wishful
selves throwing, catching, hitting, running
bases, staring with the same eyes back
and forth as pitcher and as batter.
No game plays its theater so nightly:

9. It never rains on this Wrigley Field;
in this Tiger Stadium it is
always Ebbets Field, the Polo Grounds,
Forbes Field, Griffith Stadium, Braves Field,
and Comiskey Park. Whatever's green,
it's not grass; those aren't hot dogs either;
but when we depart the old within-
Fenway of January and snow,
we find ticket stubs in our wallets.

THE NINTH INNING

1. My dog and I drive five miles every
morning to get the newspaper. How
else do I find out when the Sox trade
Smoky Joe Wood for Elizabeth Bishop?
He needs persistent demonstration
of love and approval. He cocks his
head, making earnest pathetic sounds.
Although I praise his nobility
of soul, he is inconsolable

2. when I lift my hand from his ear to
shift. Even so, after the reading
the stranger nods, simpers, and offers
to share his poems with me. Dean Gratt
confided, at the annual Death
and Retirement Gala: "Professor
McCormick has not changed: A Volvo
is just a Subaru with tenure."
Catchers grow old catching, which is strange

3. because they squat so much. "The barn is
burning, O, the barn is burning on
the hill; the cattle low and blunder
in their stalls; the horses scream and hurl
their burning manes." Jennifer remains
melancholic. Do you start to feel,
Kurt, as if you're getting it? I mean
baseball, as in the generations
of old players hanging on, the young

4. coming up from triple-A the first
of September, sitting on the bench
or pinch-running, ready for winter's
snow-plowing and cement-mixing, while
older fellows work out in their gyms
or cellars, like George "Shotgun" Shuba,
who swung a bat against a tethered
ball one thousand times a day, line drives
underneath his suburban ranchhouse.

5. By twenty twenty-eight, when K.C.
turned one hundred, eighty-three percent
of American undergraduates
majored in creative writing, more
folks had MFAs than VCRs,
and poetry had passed acrylic
in the GNP. The NEA
offered fellowships for destroying
manuscript and agreeing *"never*

6. to publish anything jagged on
the right side of the page, or *ever*
described as 'prose poems.' " Guerrillas
armed with WordPerfect holed in abstract
redoubts. Chief of Staff Vendler mustered
security forces, aka
death squads, and issued cheerful reports
nightly on lyric television.
Hideous shepherds sing to their flocks

7. under howling houses of the dog.
At the Temple Medical Center
in New Haven I wait. My mother
at eighty-six goes through the upper
and lower GI again. My mind
jangles, thinking of my sick son in
New York and his sick one-year-old girl.
This afternoon, if the x-rays go
all right, I drive back to New Hampshire.

8. In New Hampshire, late August, the leaves
turn slowly, like someone working to
order — protesting, outraged — and fall
as they must do. The pond water stays
warm but the campers have departed.
By the railroad goldenrod stiffens;
asters begin a late pennant drive
in front of the barn; pink hollyhocks
wilt and sag like teams out of the race.

9. No Red Sox tonight, but on Friday
a doubleheader with the Detroit
Tigers, my terrible old team, worse
than the Red Sox who beat the Yankees
last night while my mother and I watched
— the way we listened, fifty years back —
spritely ghosts playing in heavy snow
on VHS 30 from Hartford,
and the pitcher stared at the batter.

THE MUSEUM OF
CLEAR IDEAS

ᘒ

Or say:
Horsecollar's Odes

For the poet is light, winged, and holy. There is no inven-
tion in him until he has been inspired, out of his senses,
and has no mind.

— Socrates to Ion

Poets refuse to *utilize* language. Since the quest for truth
takes place in and by language, it is useless to imagine that
poets look for truth.

— Jean-Paul Sartre, *What is Literature?*

One morning W.B. came back from the post office. "I
don't understand," he cried. "It's closed! No one is there!"
"But Mr. Yeats," I replied, "It is Christmas Day."

— Dorothea von Kreicke, *The Swan's Wife*

I am quite deaf now. Such a comfort.

— Evelyn Waugh to Nancy Mitford

Decius — whose guileful agency sustains
and decimates me — I know that some people
require fame as athletes; still others demand
election to office or every gadget
for sale on 42nd Street; Tanaquil
enjoys dozing in the British Museum
and its pub; she prefers them to Disney World,
while her Chair, who won an all-expenses-paid
weekend in Rome, Italy, would have favored
Las Vegas. Marvin enjoys drinking himself
quadriplegic, Joan backpacks through Toledo,
Kim helicopters into Iranian
deserts, and Flaccus shoots tame wild antelope
in a hired game preserve. As Horsecollar nods,
"It takes all kinds," Madonna continues to
writhe in public, doing what she wants; Max finds
fire hydrants to piss against; Senator Hell
displays risky photographs in a cloakroom;
and Fidelia lowers her artificial
eyelashes in the direction of Tu Fu,
who sits cross-legged in his hut, composing,
oblivious that he is starving. Glaucus
urges American men to go bowling
together — to discover Mister Zero
of the bowling alley. Arbogast daydreams,
Camilla tends peonies ten hours a day,
and Julia with net and binoculars
treks through jungles and over Himalayas,
adding to her collection of deities.

I know that some people exist to look thin,
others stare at television sets all day
until they die, and others expend their lives
to redeem the dying. As for Horsecollar,
Decius, he'll take this desk, this blank paper,
this Bic, and the fragile possibility
that, with your support, the Muse may favor him.

We've come to expect earthquakes, fires, hurricanes,
and tidal waves from our whitecoated brothers
whose laboratories shed radiation
        on land and landscape,

disabling cities. Foresighted citizens
outfit granite arks in Idaho's brown hills,
stocked against flood, famine, pestilence, war, and
        hunger of neighbors,

with bulgur, freeze-dried Stroganoff, and Uzis.
Let's remember: Our great-grandfathers holed up
in mountains with pistols and pemmican, their
        manhood sufficient,

should they avoid peritonitis and gan-
grene, to perform the mechanic alchemy
which liquefied landscape, dirt to nuggets, and
        sluiced a state golden.

Let's remember not only the local wars
over claims but a late conflict of siblings
in aristocracy and the stock market,
        sharing destruction.

Or recollect the brothers who stayed back east
laboring in the shoe factory, or their
bosses who summered hunting in Scotland and
        reside forever

in the Protestant Cemetery at Rome
among cats, the pyramid of Cestius,
and Keats's grave. What use are those forefathers
        to our condition?

We want comfort: Shall we consult Jefferson?
Alas, he's busy conducting a call-in
show for Republican-Democrats. Franklin?
        He is occupied

obliterating SIN from Webster's project.
If we approach doddering George Washington,
he only smiles at us in his foolishness.
        Shall we call upon

Abraham Lincoln for succor? No: The Great
Emancipator succumbs to Grant's whiskey.
As we approach the present, passing double
        Roosevelts, we do

not help ourselves — not with old Eisenhower
cursing at caddies; not with Nixon cursing.
But if we return past Jonathan Edwards,
        past Cotton Mather,

to the Israelites of the *Mayflower* —
who make covenant with Jehovah's promised
wilderness and the manna of Indian
        corn, who stay secure

in Adam's fall and the broken promises
of the remnant — we discover ancestors
appropriate to our lapsarian state:
     Their rage sustains us.

        ଚ୭

    Or say: When we're sixty
    years old we know better
    and do less. The things we
    know better are antinomian
    adventure, sequent despair,
    error, self-deception, failure,
    and good cheer. No wonder
    that we'd prefer, with
    the dying Irish poet, to
    be "young" and "ignorant."

Let engine cowling rivets
      adhere. Let hydraulic systems operate
flaps without interruption
      and electric signals work as expected.

O 747
      that carries Glaucus across the Atlantic
and slants down over the brief
      Mediterranean to the Grecian shore,

keep him safe. Not long ago
      flying required noticeable bravery
as a bold Frenchman, not to
      say Dayton, Ohio's bicycle-making

brothers, ascended on frail
      boxes into an alien windstream, never
questioning propriety
      but taking air on challenge as their domain.

When their eyes teared with the wind,
      did they fear wind? Although they climbed the breezes
of our own century, they
      seem ancient as Leonardo or Fulton.

They were gallant without guilt
      as they rose up, and expected to return —
after ingenuity
      and courage sustained them their moment's release

from the ponderable weight
         of gravity — to accept the gratitude
of their descendants. But they
         prepared us Dresden's fire and Nagasaki's.

Are we grateful for the death
         that drops on us from flying mental engines
the Renaissance invented
         with enlightened conceit? If we beg pardon,

as we dig holes for ourselves,
         all right; but if we ascend, separated
from grief's ground without terror
         or foreboding, we add complacency to

wickedness, idiocy,
         and engineering. Fear death. Anxiety
mothers and fathers souls
         giddy with vacuum — otherwise orphaned.

Winter's asperity mollifies under the assault of April.
      Now the trout fisherman flexes stiff waders;
now cattle and sheep clamber out of barns that kept them warm all winter;
      now the countryman no longer seeks comfort

by sleeping on his Glenwood, for ice has departed the coldest field.
      Under the new moon animal bodies play,
cavorting on tender grasses that the breezes caress and embrace.
      Each morning we gaze at daffodils, closing

our eyes in languor. Soon we will inspire the July garden's densest
      effluence and shuffle to drowse in maple
shade and the shade of birches, convening where soft mosses are softest
      to build with our bodies temples for Venus

as summer suggests: We sigh, we are easy — because we understand
      that we must squeeze every moment: The truest
aphrodisiac is our certain knowledge that we will die: We sweat,
      we pant, we drop our pants whenever we touch

the subject of dying — because dead people rarely appear content;
      because they want energy; because they lack
desire for each other's bodies. In response to death's deplorable
      likelihood, we bed each other down in spring.

∞

Or say: In spring (and for that matter in summer, fall,
and winter) each of us dreadfully desires to die.
However, our conventions consider this longing morbid
and in the worst possible taste: Therefore we dress up
in costumes of lust to distract ourselves; we pound
and jab ourselves into each other — we flail, we froth,
our cup runneth over — in order to provoke blood chemistry
that, for the moment, relaxes our lust for oblivion
by substituting oblivion. As Horsecollar says, adopting
the style of his alternative Citizen Zero, "Love
and death, love and death: How do you tell them apart?"

WHO'S THIS FELLOW

Who's this fellow wearing the aftershave lotion
with the slim figure embracing you, Fidelia,
　　　in the rose garden beside
　　　　　the artificial hill?

I suppose that he's nameless and legion, for whom
you loosen your golden abundant sensuous
　　　hair. For the rest of his life
　　　　　he'll weep over this hour,

whimper himself green deploring inconstancy,
make hack metaphors that associate fickle
　　　seas with storms and dread shipwrecks —
　　　　　this same amorous boy

who sighs with pleasure now, credulous of yellow
tresses, loyalty, and unfading loveliness —
　　　ignoring the Oedipal
　　　　　weather of history.

Ridiculous that he suffers this ecstasy
over you! Horsecollar knows, who points a moral
　　　of shipwreck and survival
　　　　　as he drips saltwater.

I'm not up to it. Oh, it would require Dante
to tell your story, even Gore Vidal himself
to describe, Professor, the filth and corruption
      of your critical maneuvers!

Others drain swamps, you swamp the drains. In Manhattan,
you leave muddy crocodiles asleep where Elm Street
used to cross Maple; your depraved taste and judgment
      effect this metamorphosis.

Commissioner, how can I sing adequately
of the gross self-seeking that beats to enable
your cardiovascular system? How can I
      — pastoral, gentle, good-natured —

recount the conflicts of interest and favor-
trading that distinguish your abuses of power,
O Eulogist of Whatever Crawls on Twelve Legs?
      My petty Muse lacks energy

to reveal feculent praises supplied as blurbs
to be bartered for Guggenheims and Pulitzers.
The major industry of the Scilly Islands
      is doing each other's laundry.

∞

Or say: Ancient Maître Zero, toothless
and seamed as corduroy, sipping brandy
on Montparnasse, answers Horsecollar's
question for the *Paris Review* — "What keeps
you alive?" — with one word, and a sneer
as venerable as Tutankhamen's: "Revenge!"

Let many bad poets praise the Grand Canyon, the Panama
      Canal, the Statue of Liberty, Mount
Hood, the Napa Valley with its products of fermentation,
      Sicily, Connecticut, and themselves.

Some of us spend our whole lives praising Danbury, New Hampshire,
      or Mount Fuji: Praising our places, we
praise ourselves while pretending to look outward. We build Tu Fu's
      Chengdu cottage as a shrine for ourselves

in every *Poetry*, by printing reflections, in free verse
      without noticeable attention to
line breaks, on snapshots of the poetic mother and father,
      in their weird clothes, on vacation, before

the poet was born: How poignant it is, how remarkable
      that one's parents were older than oneself!
Then they died. Oh. Because I have nothing to say, and nothing
      deeply pitiable to whine over,

I program my poem-processor for irony, malice,
      envy, loathing, and the decent pleasure
of breaking anyone's Mont Blanc who disturbs my solitude.
      While others probe an already sore place

with the pickaxes of guilty ululation, I relax
      with a good book on the soul's wooden porch,
or, as they advised Amos some ages ago, I eat bread
      and prophesy. It happens I predict

myself, praising my villa as Horace did, praising Ragged,
Camilla, Eagle Pond, and Max the dog.
I prophesy the country I invent by shutting the door;
I praise citizenship in the nation

of myself. You too can withdraw into a granite valley
defended by the troops of history,
learning, sexual luxury, diligence, and narcissism.
Just remember: Never knock on this door.

In the name of Madonna,
        Tanaquil, why do you find it necessary to ruin
Marvin for love? Now he loathes
        the streets of his city who used to delight in running them;

Marvin goes bowling no more;
        no longer does Marvin drag-race his Buick on the back roads;
no longer does Marvin slurp
        sweet wine while playing jokers wild with pals from the department.

This was the manly Marvin
        renowned for drinking a case of Hamm's while going four for four
or making strikes with one hand
        while spilling a Seven and 7 from the hairy other.

Now he lies low, Tanaquil,
        concealing secondary sexual characteristics
that were famous. His mother
        dressed Achilles as a girl, to keep him from dying at Troy.

MOUNT KEARSARGE SHINES

Mount Kearsarge shines with ice; from hemlock branches
snow slides onto snow; no stream, creek, or river
        budges but remains still. Tonight
            we carry armloads of logs

from woodshed to Glenwood and build up the fire
that keeps the coldest night outside our windows.
        Sit by the woodstove, Camilla,
            while I bring glasses of white,

and we'll talk, passing the time, about weather
without pretending that we can alter it:
        Storms stop when they stop, no sooner,
            leaving the birches glossy

with ice and bent glittering to rimy ground.
We'll avoid the programmed weatherman grinning
        from the box, cheerful with tempest,
            and take the day as it comes,

one day at a time, the way everyone says.
These hours are the best because we hold them close
        in our uxorious nation.
            Soon we'll walk — when days turn fair

and frost stays off — over old roads, listening
for peepers as spring comes on, never to miss
        the day's offering of pleasure
            for the government of two.

Mercury, descendant of Henry Ford's five-
dollar-a-day Model-T factory line,
you educated us and provided means
       of exploration,

messenger of adult pleasures that began
at the drive-in movie and continued when
we flew ourselves out of town, winged at the heel,
       unnoticed by blue

parents or policemen, to hasten with joy
from public highways onto backroads beside
meadows with your radio playing soft tunes
       while we played also.

Helped by ingenious cherished disorder,
we resisted intimidation from old
gods and new teachers, in order to turn old
       ourselves, past sedans

and stationwagons back to the two-seater:
Oh, surely your transport will return again
in the procession of motors following
       a sable Lincoln.

Camilla, never ask when it will happen, for we'll never know
how it comes or when. Leave divination to Julia, our friend
who orders predestination from catalogues of remaindered
theologies. Let us determine to take what comes, hot or cold,
whether we stay alive into old age or drop dead next Tuesday,
which is doubtless as good a day as any. Tonight let us fill
our wineglasses without fretting about the future, which only
sours the Beaujolais. Forget tomorrow's blueberries; eat today's.

The times are propitious for fake religions.
Today let's decide which priest, beauty, athlete,
moviestar, or Jungian to celebrate
      by electing him

God. Hype springs eternal in the human breast.
Let's diversify spiritual options,
play New Age rock, and improvise jargon with
      Julia, founder

of the God-of-the-Month Club, who keeps busy
shamaning around in her medicine man
costume, afterward to go Sufi dancing
      with Jerry Falwell

outside the Zen temple just dedicated
to Kali, Martin Luther, and Orphée, who
plays for the waltzing of Mithra, Hercules,
      and Joseph Campbell

wearing his benign suit. Our bewitching friend
mumbles and invokes, imploring the oak trees
to accept worship — or should we say workshop?
      It's literary.

Polytheism pays tribute to singleness
by proclaiming Zeus CEO. Julia
has always found him authoritarian;
      if Julia feels

humble toward one god, she makes up another,
as her suburban divine rotten boroughs
grant Julia an Olympic parliament's
         perpetual rule.

Now with her biorhythm calculator,
organic vitamins, ouija board, yoga
exercises, mesmerism, Iroquois shells,
         Obeah routines,

Zen meditation, Tantric sexgames, Shirley
MacLaine, phrenology, Fletcherizing, I
Ching, and crucifix, she's in total control.
         Unless she isn't.

Gibbon published the first volumes of *Decline*
in 1776. When he praised
the Antonine who, although quite sensible,
         believed that planets

controlled destinies, he assured Jefferson
that until recently quite a few *almost*
intelligent folk believed such idiot
         junk. What sign are we,

Julia? Whatever superstitious trek
you follow today, you'll find a new Tibet
by nightfall tomorrow. Have you learned to mold
         Aztec sugarskulls?

The Apostate rises from his magician's
cave, cobwebbed and fusty, hearing your summons:
to expunge the light of the centuries' wit,
        to bring in his train

a hobgoblin horde of devils and monsters
carrying bronze tridents, disreputable
strongmen, giants, gargoyles, licentious shepherds,
        nymphs, dragons, satyrs,

saints with fake wounds, messengers — the revenant
discredited minor athletes of magic
and bêtise, rabble of nothing, who proclaim:
        "Let there be darkness."

                              ∞

Or say: The much-esteemed Gibbon and his Virginian
colleagues by cheerful error calculated
that civilization motored a tidy upward turnpike
to culminate in the city of Guess Who's worldly
intelligence. But from A.D. 300, for a millennium,
every daughter knew less than her mother, every
son less than his father. Now, as we dispute
over the exact moment when we engaged this autobahn
downward again — hurtling in a tinny Cadillac fueled
by idleness, greed, and superstition — our great-
grandfathers (the ones who could read and write)
drape themselves white to hear our diminished
chicken-cackle language in the parliament of fools.

Drusilla informs young Libo
      about her former lover's gross pectorals
and biceps. Does she want the man
      to expire of a terminal jealousy?

He shakes, his vision blurs, his skin
      whitens and turns cold; a repulsive teardrop,
unbidden and deplorable,
      slips down his cheek in evident dishonor.

Will this acknowledgment serve? When
      she adds that her thighs were bruised and blue, heaving
under her temporary hunk,
      and that his teeth marked her neck, need her Libo

roll on his back wagging his tail?
      "Please extend your constancy backward," he begs,
"removing this fellow's swart grunts
      who brutalized the body of your young skin.

"Retrospective fidelity,"
      he declares, "will obliterate earlier
error. O Drusilla, let us
      unscrew the past." "Where is my suitcase?" she says.

Ship of state, hightide rising
carries you off again, far
            from land. When you packed
                black traffic

to Virginia's shore, whole
cloth expanded under blue
            heaven. New England's
                enlightened

gentry constituted you
of stout pine and steam-bent oak
            for the seasonal
                hurricane

but not to withstand the rage
that your cargo turns on you
            as you divagate
                uncaptained

on the greedy fitful winds
of your final century.
            I beg you to sink
                abruptly.

                ∽

Or say: We catch sight of you through the rain
and wind, Yankee clipper, as the tide's

defeat carries you off your mooring and out
to sea — from the Museum of Clear Ideas
into twenty-foot waves of Atlantic rubbish.
You're unfit for traffic, *Philosophe*, which is all
you were fitted out for. Where the wind leans,
your rational rudder takes you — the wind
is your helmsman — and neither intelligence nor will
takes passage with you, who were constructed for
eternity and Philadelphia by the reasonable will.

.   .   .

Or say it as
Officer Zero:
ship of state, shit.
We assert an
historical
decline and fall
to deny our
own shipwreck. Why
does it require
sixty years to
discover that
it's the leaky
rowboat of the
self that founders
in the always
ruinous sea?

When the young husband picked up his friend's pretty wife
in the taxi one block from her townhouse for their
first lunch together, in a hotel dining room
      with a room key in his pocket,

midtown traffic gridlocked and was abruptly still.
For one moment before klaxons started honking,
a prophetic voice spoke in his mind's ear despite
      his pulse's erotic thudding:

"The misery you undertake this afternoon
will accompany you to the ends of your lives.
She knew what she did when she agreed to this lunch,
      although she will not admit it;

and you've constructed your playlet a thousand times:
cocktails, an omelet, wine; the revelation
of a room key; the elevator rising as
      the penis elevates; the skin

flushed, the door fumbled at, the handbag dropped; the first
kiss with open mouths, nakedness, swoon, thrust-and-catch;
endorphins followed by endearments; a brief nap;
      another fit; restoration

of clothes, arrangements for another encounter,
the taxi back, and the furtive kiss of goodbye.
Then, by turn: tears, treachery, anger, betrayal;
      marriages and houses destroyed;

small children abandoned and inconsolable,
their foursquare estates disestablished forever;

the unreadable advocates; the wretchedness
          of passion outworn; anguished nights

sleepless in a bare room; whiskey, meth, cocaine; new
love, essayed in loneliness with miserable
strangers, that comforts nothing but skin; hours with sons
          and daughters studious always

to maintain distrust; the daily desire to die
and the daily agony of the requirement
to survive, until only the quarrel endures."
          Prophecy stopped; traffic started.

                ∽

        Or say: Why this whining? You liked
        your nooky well enough, back when
        you had your teeth. Agreed, you
        enjoyed the performance of rage
        and disloyalty as much as orgasm;
        still, you cherished the first time
        a new one reached behind her back
        to unfasten her bra, or slipped her
        pants down hooking thumbs over black
        silk. You devoted the greatest part
        of the intelligence and energy of your
        middle years to security measures:
        maildrops, codes, and safehouses.
        Do you croon guilt's anthem now
        — after twenty years of diligence
        and a gold watch — because your bald
        agent retires from the company?

Old woman whom I remember beautiful
and young, I who am still older recollect
    words that shame me: Sink my abusive
      words under the Pacific Ocean.

Nothing is so ruinous as revenge's
rage — not whiskey, not the imagination,
    not love of country. In rage's house
      nothing rules but rage, and the waters

cannot drown it nor the winds blow it away
nor the fires burn it down. In our human minds
    ferocities gather and enlarge
      that we attempt to call inhuman:

The starved lion's hungry fury as he tears
the antelope resides in us: These rages
    destroyed Socrates and Stalingrad
      together, Masada and Emma

Bovary and Troy. Lion men burn houses
with their bushes and gardens until cities
    become cinder heaps that stink of meat.
      When I was forty animals walked

inside me. I was their cage, and when the gate
swung open I swung it. My lions loosened
    blood in the suburbs. I wrote those words
      to tear you with the five claws of rage.

It was love that grew eyeteeth, not for love bites;
it was love that made war. What other destroys
      so thoroughly as love does? Revenge
            and destruction are love's two faces.

               ∞

Or say: Yes, fucking you was terrific fun,
enlivening several months of Horsecollar's
boring midlife crisis: When you rolled over,
he never knew *what* would roll over. But when
you dumped him, Fidelia, he wasn't quite
finished. As old Horsecollar apologizes
for intemperate words uttered in impetuous
middle age, Brother Zero watches a mummified
thug crawl from its bog with a gasoline can
and matches for the house still smoldering.

When the fine days migrate east from Ohio,
climbing Vermont's greenest mountains and fording
      the Connecticut at White River
            Junction; when our meadows take relief

from inversions and July's lamentable
heat, you and I hike in fortuitous air
      up-mountain on logging roads — our dog
            Max leading us, bouncing, looking back

with mild impatience, making sure we follow —
and kneel taking joy of tiny red blossoms
      in moss. Here are no snakes to beware;
            here the shy black bear conceals himself;

here the glory of creation loosens our
spirits into appropriate surrender.
      Looking down past a clearing, we fill
            with the fullness of the valley's throat,

where the slow cattle grind the abundant grass
and their laboring stomachs turn green to white;
      where the fat sheep graze without budging,
            like soft white boulders. Now Max settles

alert, his nostrils twitching to read calm air.
Let us descend, Camilla, to the long white
      house that holds love and work together,
            and play familiar music on each

other's skin. Today we won't worry about
weather, depression, or war; about bad luck
 for our labors; about heart attacks
 or metastasis to the liver.

Nothing, my aging Flaccus, looks so happy next to your ranch
as your grape arbor, like many other domestic vineyards
here in suburban Rhode Island. Gentlemen who neglect grapes
in their daily diets, not to say fermented cereals
(our actual favorites), live depressing lives unrelieved
by vomiting, hallucination, hangover, or passing
out. In your rumpus room let us celebrate moderation
in all things. If we do not contain or control addiction,
we will not after all survive to ruin our middle age
in a continual drunken stupor, which deadens the pain
of daily depression. Let us assemble to celebrate
whiskey, wine, beer, ale, gin, rum, and the middle way. Vitamins
carefully administered will help us evade the anguish
of aging without undue attention to the suffering
we inflict (mostly upon devoted families) except
for a few alert moments before we are granted to die.

When I was young and sexual
      I looked forward to a cool Olympian age
for release from my obsessions.
      Ho, ho, ho. At sixty the body's one desire

sustains my pulse, not to mention
      my groin, as much as it ever did, if not quite
so often. When I gaze at your
      bottom as you bend gardening, or at your breasts,

or at your face with its helmet
      of sensuous hair, or at your eyes proposing
the text of our next encounter,
      my attention departs from history, baseball,

food, poetry, and deathless fame.
      Let us pull back the blanket, slide off our bluejeans,
assume familiar positions,
      and celebrate lust in Mortality Mansions.

∞

Or say: Then why does fantasy roll
Debbie Does Horsecollar, in which
he shares the screen with an idiot
teenage stranger of long blond hair
with whom he could not sustain
conversation for thirty seconds?
Although it's bully that Horsecollar
copulates as a sexagenarian
(we needn't congratulate him, Doctor
Zero notes), he must acknowledge
that the god is blind and a baby.

Flaccus, drive up from Providence to see us.
I'll buy some bargain Scotch at a New Hampshire
liquor store and we'll celebrate your new book
        and that good review

in the *New York Times*, which you'll complain about
— I don't see how — while you denounce your old friends
for their usual treacheries; but after
        two hours of kvetching

you'll quiet down; you'll begin to laugh. I know
you can do better for Scotch in Rhode Island,
but no one there puts up with your complaining.
        We miss you. Come soon.

Praise Mammon-Mazda that smartly entertains us
day and night, bringing a flat world into our eyes
      and living rooms without stink
          or terror: stainless bloodstains.

Girls, pray at pink altars to the hairless goddess;
bless the petro-divinity of your heroes,
      boys, while the whole family
          kneels at the shrine erected

by money's priests that commune to consume our hours;
bless CBS, NBC, ABC, and for
      a monthly fee bless fifty
          channels of wafer-cable.

In return for our faithfulness, we are given
the paradise of eternal distraction. Let
      other countries riot and
          starve: We'll die watching them die.

Let us meditate the virtue of slogans.
Let us declare onomastic solutions
to difficulties largely unnameable,
     and by the mottoes

of euphemism contract verbal righteousness.
Let's indite bulletins to tell everyone
the Jargon of Things, to name Lifestyles, to learn
     the Tongue of High Coy:

Do you desire to purchase a beverage?
We thank you for not smoking. Have a nice day.
May we share these suggestions with you? Let us
     praise exaltation,

never calling a route salesman a milkman,
nor an officer of the law a cop, nor
a senior citizen old, nor a starving
     freezing bagwoman

poor. When we can't alter ills that upset us,
we will change their names to prevent compassion
from disturbing our ungulate composure:
     words to deny worlds.

Vocabulary voids original sin;
cavalry of the lie reaches Calvary
just in time — to bugle Christ down from the cross.
     But: no nails, no Christ.

DON'T BE AFRAID

Don't be afraid; you look scared, like Max the wimpy
dog who leaps to escape the just-glimpsed attacking
        puffball. Max defends the lintel
                fiercely, but a sudden windstorm

reduces him to whimpering in a corner;
or a green beetle, doubtless with an expression
        of malevolence, sets his fur
                ruffling into the attack mode.

We promise never to stuff and mount his handsome
head over the fireplace, nor yours either. Calm down.
        Timidity encourages
                death and never prevents dying.

We explore grief's borders, boundaries of mourning
and lamentation, wild cries and unending tears,
when the unexpected and unacceptable
      death happens. Henry King, teach us

to grieve with gratitude, who mourned for your young wife
in a Christian elegy. It is our habit
to continue by daydream to contradict death,
      so that continually we

imagine our friend smiling to hear our stories
or taking pleasure in some piece of good fortune
until her death leaps out of the corner again
      to jeer at us: *No, no, you don't!*

The whole village weeps. Where shall we take our pleasures
for validation? Houses and farms and hamlets
mourn her absence, and no one more than Camilla,
      who studied, watching her, the craft

of growing old with dignity and amusement.
Still we dream to whisper: "The coast is clear. Please come
out! This underground business has lasted too long:
      Relent. Relent. Relent. Relent."

∾

Or say: All tears
weep for the weeper.
The tissue that dries
our eyes is a clear
understanding that this
disappearance we
complain of will drop
oblivion's lid
over us soon enough.

I suppose you've noticed, Fidelia, that drunks
rarely bang on your door anymore. You sleep
straight through, no longer aroused every few hours
     by an amorous

clamor. Your telephone no longer jangles
at three A.M., breathes in your ear, and hangs up.
No more does your latest victim, or maybe
     the victim before

last, wake you by asserting that you're heartless
for sleeping while he dies, much worse by sleeping
with someone else. If it was unfair that your
     lovers tormented

you for your beauty, cheer up: Worse suffering
derives from age's ruin. It's not your fault
that your skin puckers, sags, and gathers, but now
     men turn away when

you expect homage. When you lust — lust never
relents — your wet fury finds no complaisant
organ. You whine; you drink vodka; and your old
     lovers groan: revenged.

                ᔍ

Or say: If your old lovers consider
their anguish revenged because
you suffer as they did, nonetheless
they dupe themselves, fixing doddery
eyes on women who ignore them. Revenge,
as Comrade Zero takes pains to observe,
is reflexive: Youth considers age
reproof for survival. Eld understands
that retribution will gather, crazed
as old porcelain, at the corners
of beautiful young eyes and mouths.

I celebrate myself. It's intelligent
to compound one's natural ability
      by hard work and luck, don't all of us
            agree? I sing in praise of Horsecollar,

complacently, without fear of murderous
rivals. I sing to display my Alcaics
      and my nobility of spirit:
            I praise friends engaged in the same project

and implore the Muses that have favored me
to set resplendent laurels on the heads of
      Flaccus, Camilla, and Arbogast:
            "Parnassus affords adequate housing."

∽

      Or say: Mania like despair
      is doubtless useful to poets
      but grossly unreliable as
      an index to reality. Like the
      late Lamont Cranston, Captain
      Zero *knows:* Horsecollar, if you
      don't fear murderous rivals,
      better cringe in a safehouse
      under some Disney pseudonym.

Arbogast, can you call to mind that night when
you and I, engaged in some disputation,
            broke wineglasses on each other's heads?
                        We resembled passionate Englishmen

then, rather than the correct, upright, pious
New England poets we intended to be.
            Now we become *mature*, don't we now?
                        Grapes contribute to civilization

in the tradition of reasonable joy,
as we learned in our prepschool years long ago,
            among the young imperialists
                        against whom we measured our excellence.

What's this? You tell me to pipe down and drink up?
Suppose you try talking without slurs, and *then*
            give me orders. O.K., I won't speak
                        of your fifty years; instead, I'll question

your reasons for complaining: What's wrong with you?
What is it that you want that you can't have? Oh,
            I bet you're lovesick again. Shocking!
                        Will you tell the object of your desire?

To be nympholeptic again — at your age!
I despair of detaching you from raptures
            of misery; you seem to enjoy
                        Circe's sty . . . But no, it's Penelope's!

                        ∞

Or say: If a friendship of decades can survive
the madness of old age, it can survive treachery,
murder, and even, possibly, another's success.

Sabina — who explored internal continents for decades
of poetry, bourbon, and night — molders
in a patch of Oregon far from her Vermont. For thirty
years she made poems out of her troubles

and places — out of Middlebury, West Los Angeles, and
Happy Valley — poems that stay alive
years after her early death. But Sabina was born to die
like her poetic mothers and fathers,

like the sisters and brothers of our more ordinary lives
and would-be making. Even the great ones?
Maybe great ones especially die. We the still surviving
belittle ourselves at the funerals

of genius that offered us pause. We understand that we will
also die, but claim, or wish to believe,
that women and men who appear to stop time by their products
never depart entirely from being.

Nonetheless, Sabina disintegrates in her bare graveyard —
as much as airline pilots whose planes crash,
or sailors who drown, or the greater number of us who stop
breathing and turn blue in attended beds.

*

When Sabina is remembered, in ten or a hundred years,
lovers and poets will visit her grave
where the Oregon dead plow their acreage. And when I die
(Horsecollar brings up someone else's death

in order to consider his own), I wish and suppose that
    my bones will disintegrate at the edge
of Proctor Cemetery under pinetrees, by ferns, with pale
    birches hovering near. After a few

years Camilla will settle alongside, if as seems likely
    we die in bed at Eagle Pond rather
than spiraling seven miles into the Pacific from holes
    in airplanes or sweeping from a wet deck

off the coast of Maine. Possibly pious descendants will plant
    a rose bush there. If others wish to pray
for these bones, Horsecollar thanks them gratefully from the bottom
    of his precariously beating heart.

୬

        Or say: Good master Horsecollar
        At Dartmouth-Hitchcock and in terror
        Removed a carcinoma, D. V.
            Timor mortis conturbat me.

        Sabina died ten years ago.
        Flaccus endures, Death's sworn foe,
        As Marvin burns melanoma away.
            Timor mortis conturbat me.

        Kim died of the cure. My old teacher
        Inhaled a carton of throat cancer
        And each generation learns to die.
            Timor mortis conturbat me.

Fran was the first: She was run over;
Glaucus leapt underearth for cover.
Great ruth it were that it should be.
   Timor mortis conturbat me.

∞

Or say it as
Master Zero:
Praise self-pity;
if it were not
for copious
resources of
this indulgence,
doubtless old men
would engage no
feelings at all.

Flaccus, Camilla, Decius, Arbogast:
Do we determine our lives or suffer them?
            Tanaquil, did you make yourself up
                    out of whole cloth or from reading *Plotto?*

It is less wearing, and less time-consuming,
to daydream adventures than to run through them
            as if we trotted among land mines.
                    What else is literature for besides

avoidance of life? (Whatever we intend
by "life" this week.) Books are more manageable
            than griefs, so marry a book; follow
                    invented pages back into childhood

where we become more charming rather than less,
where our soft skin grows rosy and less wrinkled,
            where all things, especially desires,
                    remain safely (and merely) potential.

O Camilla, is it conceivable that
you feel as ardent as I do — as horny
as seven goats? Camilla, let us hurry
        out of these grossly

getting-in-the-way clothes onto a wide bed
with its covers hurled off to play skin-music
on bright sheets, slowly increasing the tempo
        until Eden comes.

           ∞

Or say: At this moment, according to habit,
Horsecollar interrupts his ode to contradict
his ode; or calls upon Professor Zero to sneer
at Horsecollar, at hypocritical humanity, and at
Professor Zero. Analysands cherish reversals
in the performance of Heraclitean understanding
achieved after eight years on a Viennese sofa;
Horsecollar revels in luxuries of antithesis,
by which any Eden, temperate with blessedness,
freezes forever in the flames of coldest hell.

It was Sigmund Freud, I believe, who inquired:
"What is it that poets want?" We understand
    that magic thinking is fundamental,
        but what does poetic magic ask for?

Not riches nor whiskey nor satyrs nor nymphs;
not real estate, not pure Acapulco gold,
    not a journey to the Galápagos,
        not French dinners that cost a year's wages.

All of these diversions, heaven knows, appeal
to poets as much as to anybody,
    but not to poets *as* poets. People
        in Cambridge, Mass., and Iowa City,

educated cynics, tell us that poets
are just as corrupt as they are, which may be
    true — but if corruption were the only
        criterion, why aren't *they* poets?

Crooked or straight, poets mortgage their prospects
for an improbable goal: to make objects
    carved in the abiding stone of language;
        to leave, when they die, durable relics.

                  ര

Or say: They defecate petrified horsemanure. They create:
lifelong hatred derived from a moment's disparagement;
murderous envy; suicidal despair; desperate and ingenious
politicking. As Horsecollar praises psychic ambivalence,
he reaffirms commitment to lifelong heartfelt narcissism
and offers himself (who else?) the sincere consolation
above. It is worth observing that it requires only a cubic
centimeter of the proper elements, in proportion, to drive
ambition's spaceship a million miles an hour a thousand years
to the farthest galaxy at the temperature of Commander Zero.

"Go write a poem about it." Dutiful
Horsecollar, hastening to obey, invokes
the male Muse and tutelar of Parnassus:
        "Peter Mark Roget,

"breathe in for this inarticulate maker
of the temporary verb; supply language
as he makes up strophes fit to be counted
        Parnassian song.

"Figure him help from Brooklyn, from Cumberland
Street's wiry spinster if not the yawpmaster;
not the campy ocean but a syllabic
        exactitude, O

"numerical testudo of Athena!"
By administration of your amplitude,
Horsecollar counts on his eleven fingers
        beautiful numbers.

               ∾

    Or say: Dutiful numbers
    multiply numbers of rage.
    Horsecollar affects this
    Byzantine dialect with
    the ressentiment
    endemic to age, lifting an
    eyebrow — Chancellor Zero
    explains — superciliously.

Don't let it bother you, Flaccus, that Kimberly
dumped you for a younger chap — but stop this whining;
this blubbering cacophony is repulsive
              and self-pity requires strangling.

You say she promised? Drusilla complains of Marve,
who in his turn laments over Fidelia, who
will enter his sheets as soon as hollyhocks per-
              form sexual intercourse with

horses. Aphrodite, provoking erectile
tissue, enjoys the consternation she contrives
by engendering unreciprocal desires.
              We become friezes of pursuit.

Even Horsecollar, in his youthful days sometimes
sought after, developed erotic ambition
toward Bubbles the Body — as when the glass village
              lusted for Hurricane Venus.

Horsecollar is rarely given to worship
these days, unless we understand his mirror
      an altar before which he pauses
            in prayers of reasonable self-love.

But Horsecollar turns atheist of himself
when the lightning bolt (we openly employ
      primitive natural symbolism)
            ravages from a sky without clouds.

We accept good luck as if it were normal.
When it comes to cancer or car accidents,
      we look for malevolent design.
            Horsecollar's piety is dreadful

or selfish. Bad luck's up side is suffering,
for cheerfulness lacks social utility;
      always appropriate, misery
            on occasion generates virtue.

When the goddess Fortuna removes her mask
she becomes the Ayatollah Khomeini:
    And we are hostages to Fortune
        whether we live lucky in Loma

Linda or superior in sin, homeless
in Arcadia or six Arcadians
    to a room the size of a closet.
        We think by magic; by this magic

we avoid thinking. Atheists address prayers
to the pantheon as they sit in airport
    snack bars with vodka at eight A.M.,
        and as the overtaxed bus struggles

along the runway hold their breath, their eyes closed,
to keep wavery wings in place by voodoo.
    Oh, gangsters retailing crack cocaine,
        mothers watching their children to school,

infantrymen carrying gas masks as they
advance into Kuwaiti deserts behind
    tanks in the battle to liberate
        petroleum, tyrants whose firebombs

burn the hill tribes, each tyrant's aged mother,
the mothers of the starving tribes, the rebels
    who gather to kill the same tyrant,
        and *their* mothers — all cross damp fingers.

If we complain that Fortune is changeable,
we may attend on Necessity instead,
        also female, whose chief attribute
                is her final unchangeableness.

Necessity widowed the queen and orphaned
the beggar's daughter. Necessity differs
        from Fortune by tense: We don't expect
                to prevent what's already happened.

Necessity preserved Caesar when he struck
Englishmen at the edge of the universe
        while good fortune protected our troops
                waiting in Saudi Arabia

for the battle later called a turkeyshoot.
By technology's valor and by valor's
        dollar, without devotion we rule
                the universe of central heating.

                        ∾

        Or say: We bow to luck, constructing
        chapels of superstition to evade
        holiness and worship that terrify us
        in fragments of Christmas and Easter.

Welcome back home, Libo. Exiled
      among confederates you lived too far away
too long. Tonight we celebrate
      your return to the crimson city of Cambridge.

Drinking Samuel Adams ale
      we party all night, singing and dancing, turning
the clumsy brick streets boisterous
      in accord with lively Puritan tradition.

Drusilla with her yards of hair
      waltzes until she wears a hole in the dancefloor.
Kimberly, who drinks like a Finn,
      embraces us with general avidity.

Colonial sparrows warble
      in maples over our heads. Roses that bloomed once
bloom again, peonies fire off,
      and we roister all night under fortunate stars.

All night, Libo dancing checks out
      Drusilla sideways: so lavishly beautiful,
and so dazzled by her new beau
      that she clings to him as ivy clings to maples.

Nunc est bibendum. To condescend the phrase
into the preferred demotic — Latin that
      plain folks talk, picking up Anglish from
          the cowboy and High Dutch from the sergeant —

we may translate the suggestion, "Let's get burnt,"
or choose the style of C. E. Bennett (Cornell
      University, nineteen fourteen):
          "Now is the time to drain the flowing bowl."

However you say it, let us grab this hour
to float glorious magenta peonies
      in blue bowls on festival tables
          as we gather to cherish victory.

Until this afternoon, it seemed unlucky
to break out the cider we pressed last autumn.
      We feared that Senator Hell might win,
          wagging his sullied tail to celebrate

fund-raising, bigotry, merde, contempt for art,
and detestation of the First Amendment.
      Fundamental J. Virtue, D.D.,
          joined forces with Representative Roar

and tobacco's senator to assemble
checks and attention by denouncing poets,
      homosexuals, painters, Marxists,
          thieves, violinists, and people like that

except for Andrew Wyeth. They lost the vote
and their boats burn in the harbor. Let us drink
    to the survival of liberty —
        but remain vigilant: The enemy

always survives, for Egyptian solutions
don't wash in Washington. Senator Hell knows
    no humiliation in defeat:
        He sniffs, looking for something to roll in.

I, too, dislike it — the mannerism of plain,
natural, or idiomatic language
McPoets go in for. Horsecollar prefers
        chatting in Latin,

"Iowa delenda est," par exemple.
Squish the demotic underfoot, Arbogast.
When you take up syntax and semicolons,
        then show me your stuff.

∞

Or say: Rain on the weatherman who announces that
"we may experience shower activity" while others
claim that "it looks like rain" and Horsecollar
grumbles about "pluviosity." Now Libo disappears
from the pages of his existence, as void as Sabina
or Tu Fu who composes and decomposes together
with Camilla, Glaucus, atque Fidelia of syllabic
prurient fantasy. Horsecollar occupies his mornings
with a chisel, concentrating his stylus on language,
cutting square letters into stone, to avoid thinking
about aging, death, sexual loss, the countryside's
vanishing, replacement of affection by greed,
Mister Zero's prophylactic smirking dog-cynicism,
betrayals of love, and disappearance of the good
mothers and sisters, brothers and fathers, into dirt.

◆

EXTRA
INNINGS

◆

1. My friend David tells me that Jasper Johns
never takes his advice, so when David
suggests "Extra Innings," K.C. picks up
a bat. Last April the Boston Red Sox
beat Toronto opening day, then lost
three straight. At least, Kurt, the season started,
and even losing three out of four is
preferable to off-season — as life
despite its generic unpleasantness
appears under almost all conditions

2. more attractive than its alternative.
Batter up. We know what wins in the end,
in "Extra Innings." Therefore, many folks
settle for conditions of middleness,
lukewarm descending as far as lukecold,
pitch neither high nor low, volume neither
loud nor soft. Without a life, who fears death?
Even the season is out of season
unless we relish baseball, daydreaming
a game each night; then the morning paper.

3. After the bald surgeon making his rounds
removed the bandage from Jennifer's neck,
he pressed tiny bandaids over drainholes
side by side like snakefang punctures. As we
drove home we sat together in silence,
touching each other lightly, as if touch
were safety. Our ecstatic young dog leapt
to see her home — and pawed her incision
open. All night I reached in the darkness
to feel her familiar body again

4. and at dawn brought coffee to her bedside
as ever. All morning we sought comfort
in the blessedness of the resumed hour,
in the dear repetition of daily
gestures and tasks. We breathed calmly again
until like a sudden front from the north
we remembered the word cancer. That night,
while baseball lingered on the set, my mind
reran the last days, as a crow returns
to the perfume of putrescent carcass:

5. The drive to the hospital, admissions,
gown, bed, and a quick night's arduous sleep.
At six-thirty the following morning
I walked by her gurney to the metal
swoon of the elevator, then returned
to this house to wait for the surgeon's call.
In dread of consciousness I dozed beside
the telephone; I dreamt of a garden
where tomatoes sagged erupting black juice,
where squash lapsed softly drooling corrupt lymph

6. and seed, where Kentucky Wonders curled up,
cankered, and dropped from the derelict vine.
When the phone rang with the surgeon's message,
I would not have anyone else tell her:
I drove to the hospital to tell her
that the growth in her neck was malignant —
and that pathology's slow slides required
six days to deliver a prognosis
on the likelihood of metastasis
or probability of recurrence.

7. The entire history of human thought,
Western and Eastern, remembers and codes
our efforts to declare the real unreal.
Kurt, I almost forgot about baseball:
How would the Red Sox fare with the Yankees?
In my contracted heart Jennifer died
a thousand times. As I watched her alive,
I held her dying. Again and again,
I looked covertly at the small bandage
over the smooth skin I kissed so often

8. while we made love and I nuzzled her neck —
the skin swollen, with its row of stitches
like a zipper — and I trembled, dreading
that a black cell divided and split there.
In self-pity I watched the widower
weep by her grave: lamenting, lamented.
Sometimes a manager in a tight game
brings in a new relief pitcher for each
batter, two or three in a row — left, right,
left; meanwhile the other team's manager

9. answers with his pinch hitters — right, left, right —
after each pitcher faces one batter
until somebody runs out of bodies
on the bench or arms in the bullpen. Kurt,
do you know what a bench is? a bullpen?
Pathology telephoned its words: "a
muco-epidermoid carcinoma,
the size of a grape, intermediate
in virulence, encapsulated in
the membrane of the salivary gland" —

10. with no likelihood of metastasis
and little for recurrence. Next morning,
we woke alert in the pink-and-green dawn,
aware of joy at waking for the first
morning in weeks, in blissful consciousness
cherishing the settlement of the day:
Routine was paradise — walking the dog,
newspaper, coffee, love, rye toast, work, grape
juice, the Yankees beaten three straight, Cleveland
coming to town for four, a big series.

1. In nineteen ninety, Kurt, I picked the Red Sox
for fourth and they won the East. (But let's forget
the Oakland playoffs.) In nineteen ninety-one,
when I daydreamed before opening day that
the Red Sox took the World Series, we started
by losing four out of five. Baseball — the Sport
of Hope and Resignation: "Wait till next year."
"Next year we'll be dead, thanks; let's win it this year."
K.C. has been posthumous for twenty years
like everybody else in the universe.
The first time I died I was forty, whining

2. commonplace miseries of whiskey and love
as the Tigers kept winning; in a blurry
fury of bourbon I cheered Denny McLain
and Mickey Stanley on. Two innings ago,
at the end of the ninth, I drove my mother
for the upper GI. We dreaded cancer;
but I felt fatigued all day, taking six naps,
and it was I who constructed a quiet
carcinoma at the top of my colon.
The posthumous recognize each other at
store or postoffice: *that* one, with the pale shroud

3. wound invisibly around her body, who
exudes an aroma of continual
termination in a sickroom of terror
and gratitude. We nod at each other; we
acknowledge pain, baseball, lethargy, and cracks
in the bedroom ceiling. Do you remember
the Poverty Year of eighteen sixteen? Crops
froze twelve months out of twelve; we hungered all year
whether the Red Sox provisioned our daydreams
or froze them black. Now in the mild risen sun
we take deliberate pleasure breathing air;

4. every hour of our lives we inhale deeply
to reassure ourselves that lungs still expand
and contract. In the day we smell horsemanure
or lilac, we feel sun or hail equally,
with indifferent skin so long as synapses
fire. If a worm nibbles at the underside
of tissue, never mind: It is zero to
zero, the eleventh inning of a blue
April day. The posthumous never complain.
Kurt, I begin to understand what matters
in this daily game. Listen: Baseball is types

5. of continuousness, simultaneous
hours not consecutive ones, independent
temporalities that gather ongoing
moments into a perpetual present
that invalidates the inexorable
business of clocks. (Copy, *Sports Illustrated*.)
Five hundred years before Jesus and Caesar,
Xenophanes of Colophon recounted
what strangers said to each other, "fit topics
for conversation among men reclining
at the wineshop after a meal." The doctor

6. with thick glasses and cheerful manner mumbled,
"Fine, all clear," during the colonoscopy —
then quieted. Withdrawing his instrument,
solemn, he spoke with a summoned dignity,
looking in my eyes: "You have colon cancer,"
September 18, 1989, and
we contracted a surgeon and a schedule.
I still hear his clear inadmissible voice.
Over the season, games are quotidian
from the morning paper through extra innings
from the West Coast — fading with the pale grasses

7. of October, returning with the yellow-
green of April — measuring a timelessness
day by day and as dayless as paradise,
lacking the hour: "Before Adam was I am."
Lung cancer killed my father at fifty-two.
"A stranger asks: 'What is your family name?
How old were you when the Persians invaded?' "
Six months later, Kurt, we sat at the bedside
of Jack Jensen as he lay dying, mid-March,
while spring training thawed under Florida sun
and snow darkened by New London Hospital.

8. As his breaths grew quicker, abrupt and panicked
even in sleep, he woke smiling to offer
assurance, showing affection by smiling
because he could no longer speak. As I held
his cold hand, I felt my own hand turning cold.
My pulse slowed and energy flowed from my hand
into his hand, under blue skin to his heart;
my breath turned shallow and my dying body,
in pain of cold and good estate, drained itself
into his body. Frightened, watching my grave
open and suggest that I might enter it,

9. as if an owed death assumed me to itself,
I withdrew my hand. I warmed my aching hand
in my other hand still warm, and paced outside
his room on squares of the hospital hallway
while my friend in his pale skin snored into death.
We lay on the same bed, but I stepped away
from Jack in my fear. I prayed for forgiveness,
and next morning ate peanut butter again
for breakfast, read the *Globe*, and wrote at my desk.
When wrinkled flesh warmed itself again, I made
love with Jennifer in her grieving body.

10. In the apothegm of Baltimore Earl Weaver,
"This ain't football; we play this game every day."
Each day twenty-five men, older and younger,
throw, hit, catch, run, circle the bases; they take
BP, run wind-sprints, do infield, play pepper,
sign autographs, and chatter with young women
who lean over the dugout. Then they are old,
although they believed it would never happen:
They sell used cars, real estate, and insurance;
they pray, they eat peanut butter, they weep tears;
they practice love, sleep, work, cancer, and baseball.

11. When you drove me back home from the hospital,
you had strung tiny lights over the painted
Victorian bed. I slept. For the Series,
we moved a recliner in front of the box.
Over the weeks as I grew stronger, as pain
diminished, brother dread kept vigil by me.
But slowly the day returned; my skin returned
to rub against your skin and we touched again
in the complacency of the ecstatic
day's routine, inhabiting this clapboard,
quotidian, rare, sensible paradise.

1. Before lights, Kurt, baseball games were sometimes delayed
on account of darkness. Usually, as I
remember, they were continued and concluded
before another game began. On occasion,
now, games are suspended because of a curfew.
Really, who can finish a series like this one?
Therefore I declare that this Merzball game will stop
after twelve innings of play — although, as Nolan
Ryan puts it, pitching for Advil, "Ah could *pitch*
another *nine innings*." In nineteen fifty-five,
the Dodgers beat the Yankees in the World Series
for the first time, as Johnny Podres won three games.

2. I watched with my father on a seven-inch screen,
borrowed from a neighbor's attic, in the guest room
where he coughed toward his death on a hospital bed.
He was happy — we were happy — minutes on end,
despite the losses of voice, eyesight, and hearing.
Winning distracted us; we looked for distraction.
Kurt, did you ever observe Dr. Naismith's game?
Basketball is the performance of miracles —
levitation, luck, opposites turning into
each other, primary-process as sports event —
while baseball remains the alternative to days:
twilight on the porch, lemonade, and sleepiness.

3. Dock Ellis performed pointguard for his high school team
but pitched for a profession. He threw a no-no
for Pittsburgh against San Diego — on acid,
having forgotten that he was supposed to pitch
until almost too late. Years later Gene Clines told
the story of Dock's change-up that a prospect swung

through so humiliatingly he was finished —
sent back to triple-A, never heard from again.
In-your-face is more common in basketball, where
wonders and stunts are ordinary, good-natured,
and devastating. When we fake this way, fake that,
break past the body leaping midair to block us,

4. and lay it up behind his back, we are deathless.
Among enormous bodies, alert eyes, and hands
that flap like manta rays, dandy delicate guards
are minnows outwitting whales, or sons their fathers,
and basketball is Austrian psychodrama —
expressionist in its distortion of physics,
grand-operatic in its bipolarity —
while baseball is De Stijl: orderly, obsessive,
the meeting ground of arithmetic and beauty
or the daily grid of manic pastoral song.
In September the Red Sox have an outside chance
if Toronto keeps on clutching, if the Tigers

5. lose games they ought to lose. Today as the leaves fall
red and amber, our town's yellow schoolbus returns
up the gravel road in a mild September rain
for the waiting child who wears her yellow slicker
and carries last year's beat-up Big Bird lunchbox, first
day of school. Chill nights at Fenway bring April back
with annual ironies of remembered dreams
and retrospective foresight — as gardens go down
behind the house, under the hill. Here Jennifer
last spring raised a wild dazzlement of daffodils,
and under the high sun of July prodigious
peonies of privacy, whiter than winter;

6. where buttercups flourished by a stony wellhead,
now dry stalks wither. Hurricane Bob shut Fenway
two days in a row, pity, with Cleveland in town.
On Jennifer's neck it is impossible to
detect the scars of her cancer: virgin again.
K.C. monitors a possible recurrence
by checking the level of his blood's CEA
each quarter, raising anxiety to lose it
for three months more of Jennifer's shorts, poetry,
and baseball. My father is thirty-five years dead,
buried on Christmas Eve. For twenty years his death
provoked the choices of my life. I use mornings

7. to work in, and afternoons for reading and love,
and do desultory chores nights during baseball —
paying bills, dictating letters. When the Red Sox
play on the West Coast, K.C. takes an evening nap,
eight-thirty to ten-thirty, then watches the game
until one A.M. Five drugs together control
Jennifer's depression: She can't sleep or hold still
or watch baseball but her mood is enterprising;
joyously she writes poems that render despair
and gardens until dark encloses the garden.
She weeps to recall Jack, who turned into ashes,
remembered by a granite bench with flowering shrubs.

8. It is the season for blackberries that prosper
at roadside in thorny tangles and in the trench
of the abandoned railroad. Mrs. Roberts walks
from early spring to late fall by the asphalt's edge,
toting a Shaker basket for wild strawberries
and volunteer asparagus, for dandelion

greens in spring, for blackberries from August into
hard frost. David inquires: What does K.C. stand for
(besides the vainglorious Irishman Casey
mocked by the millowner's Harvardman son and heir)?
Prizes for best answers: Kurt Carcinoma? Kid
Chumpleheart? Kitsch Champion? Kitchen Cat? Kup Cake?

9. Steve Blass was a control pitcher one year, the next
season — after his friend Roberto Clemente's
plane crashed in a winter sea — couldn't throw a strike.
John Singer Sargent defined a portrait as "that
form of painting in which there is always 'something
a little *wrong* about the mouth.' " When I was young,
I covered my mouth when I felt a difficult
subject approach — or when I lied; with age I stopped
lying. Kurt, while you built your Merz-house, the Dodgers
played the game of baseball with Red Barber's guidance,
who still talks baseball for NPR on Fridays
from Tallahassee. His voice was soft and nervous,

10. his affection luminous. Baseball is better
than model airplanes, and poems are better still —
preferable to conceited demonstrations
that poems cannot exist and authors are dead.
Blass lost his control because he was terrified
of hitting batters — after his friend's plane went down.
He said he felt like Secretariat: all that
money and he couldn't get it up. Next year Blass
sold class rings to Connecticut high school seniors.
The farmhouse where we live straggles back to Ragged
Mountain from an ox path that became the Grafton
Turnpike in 1803, later Route 4. The cape,

11. in its almost two hundred years of adjustment
and generation, wandered from yellow to red
to white and green on the same squared-off oaken sills.
Our unpainted barn remains upright. Beside it
my grandfather and I threw baseballs back and forth
in nineteen forty-two while firebombs descended
on England, Spitfires shot down Messerschmitts, and you
coughed beginning slow death. In September maples
turn yellow and red against the black-brown rusty
barnboards; now Jennifer's sunflowers feed the autumn
chickadees, nuthatches, and slate-colored juncos;
soon grosbeaks with yellow chests will peck at the seeds.

12. In September the Red Sox lose games in the ninth.
The season ends. Even if you win the Series,
the season ends, O, and games dwindle to Florida's
Instructional League where outfielders without wheels
learn to be catchers. From Florida north will truck
oranges that Jennifer squeezes in the cold
light of a low sun. I wear my yellow sweater;
we eat scrambled eggs from blue and white dishes; her
hair's kerchief is yellow. We gather yellow days
inning by inning with care to appear careless,
thinking again how Carlton Fisk ended Game Six
in the twelfth inning with a poke over the wall.

NOTES

Another Elegy

From *The Norton Anthology of Contemporary Verse:*

"Many critics consider William Trout (1927–1977) the best poet of his crowded generation. His work followed a template common to his peers, beginning with commitment to formal ironies, departing into an asymmetric 'Blue Rider' period, and before his death reaching a new synthesis of narrative reminiscence with elements of fantasy. His books begin with *Memory's Jargon* (1956), and include *The Woodchuck and St. Ignatius* (1959), *Apples of Nightmare* (1963), *Mammal Dignity* (1970), *Another Elegy* (1972), and *Catching Bullheads in Rajasthan* (1977). The posthumous *Collected Poems* (1981) contains new and previously unprinted work.

"Born in Pocatello, Idaho, Trout grew up in the Depression, one of four brothers. His mother cooked for an Italian restaurant. (She was of Calabrian ancestry; see Trout's early 'Sabato's Taverna Tercets.') His father was a brakeman for the Union Pacific, active in the Railway Engineers' Brotherhood. (Trout's grandfather, a lumberman in Oregon, had belonged to the Industrial Workers of the World; see 'Joe Hill to Utah.') On a scholarship, Trout attended the University of Oregon in Eugene, where he edited the literary magazine and was elected to Phi Beta Kappa. On graduation he entered a seminary to train for the priesthood, but after eighteen months quit to undertake an MFA at the University of Iowa. Other students included Philip Levine, W. D. Snodgrass, Jane Cooper, Robert Bly, and Donald Justice; among his teachers were Paul Engle, Robert Lowell, and John Berryman. For an account of these early years, see Trout's lecture 'Capes and Cages,' reprinted in *Last Lost Words*, University of Michigan Press, 1981.

"Trout led a troubled life, more like the generation of his teachers than his own generation. After initial success — his Yale Younger Poets book, *Memory's Jargon,* was the Lamont Poetry Selection — he continued to publish, first with Macmillan and later with Knopf, but with interstices caused by alcoholism, drugs, and instability. In a healthy and vigorous period he worked for civil rights; later he spent months in two hospitals for the mentally ill. He received two Guggenheims. In 1969 he settled in Bolinas, teaching at the University of San Francisco. During his third marriage, to the Bengali dancer Reba Hejmadi, he wrote the poems critics find his best, especially during the final year of his life when the couple traveled extensively in Europe and India. *Catching Bullheads in Rajasthan* won a posthumous Pulitzer Prize. In the years since his death, editors have collected three volumes of essays about Trout's work; a biography is in preparation."

*

Geoffrey Hill quotes Coleridge, from *The Notebooks*, in a note to "Poetry as 'Menace' and 'Atonement' " in *The Lords of Limit* (London, 1984), 161.

Baseball

Gerald Burns suggested a poem called "Baseball"; David Shapiro, reading "Baseball," asked for "Extra Innings."

Kurt Schwitters (1887–1948), the great Dada collagist, founded his own artistic movement called *Merz*, the name taken from a fragment of an advertisement for *Commerz*. In addition to his collages, he built his own living places into sculptural assemblages, each called *Merzbau*. He escaped Germany for Norway in 1937 and emigrated to England in 1940.

The Museum of Clear Ideas

Horace Horsecollar, a minor character in Walt Disney comics, in these verses counts both Fidelia and Julia as three-syllable words. Lacking Latin, he follows his master visually — the number and shape of stanzas in Horace's first book of odes — except that Horace's fifth ode uses four stanzas; Horsecollar's "Who's this fellow" adds another.

Occasionally, after a printer's device, there is a rejoinder beginning "Or say." These verses lack an Horatian provenance.